Music Minus One
Student Series

MMO
4102

For Song Location See
Back Cover Of The Fo

MUSIC MINUS ONE Alto Sax

Easy Solos

4102

Piano Accompaniments By
HARRIET WINGREEN

Student Series

Easy ALTO SAX Solos

Volume 2

I AIN'T GONNA STUDY WAR NO MORE

Moderato ♩ = 84

Traditional

4102

THE SIDEWALKS OF NEW YORK

Charles B. Lawlor

6 taps (2 meas.)
precede music.

Waltz tempo ♩ = 168

CRADLE SONG

Johannes Brahms

Slowly ♩ = 69

ON TOP OF OLD SMOKY

MR. FROG WENT A-COURTING

Traditional

WHEN I WAS SINGLE

Traditional

FIREPROOF POLKA

Joseph Strauss

OLD PAINT

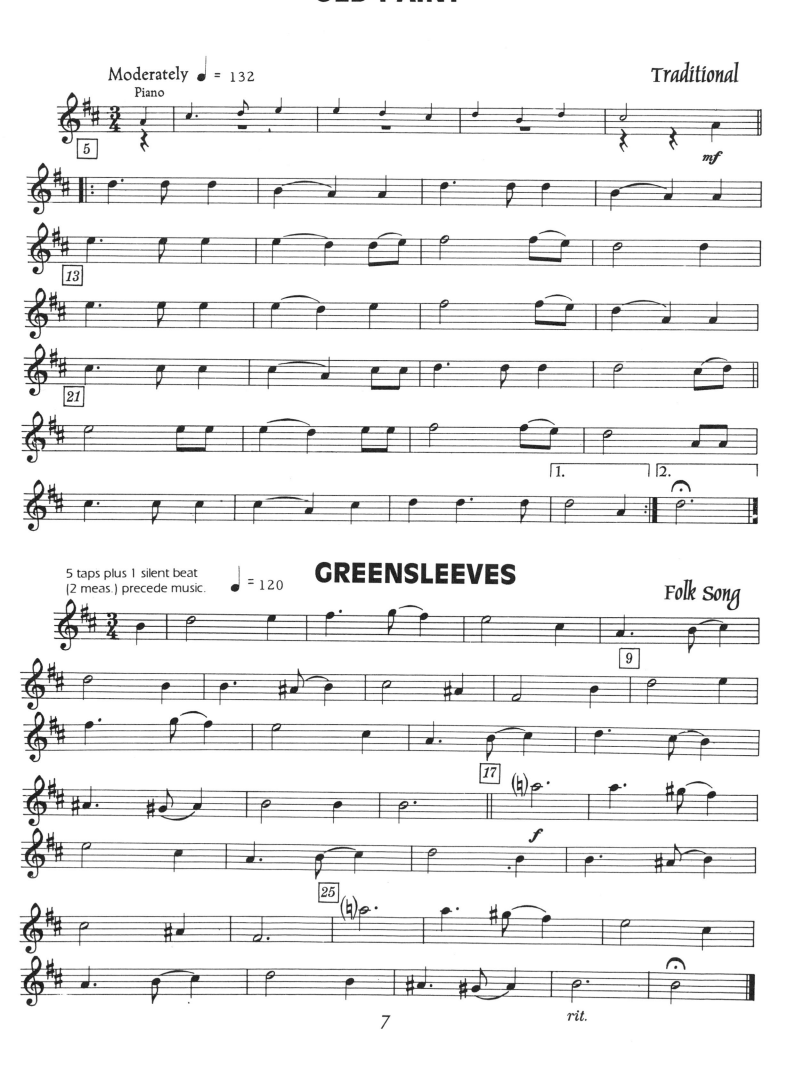

GREENSLEEVES

YOU TELL ME YOUR DREAM

Charles N. Daniels

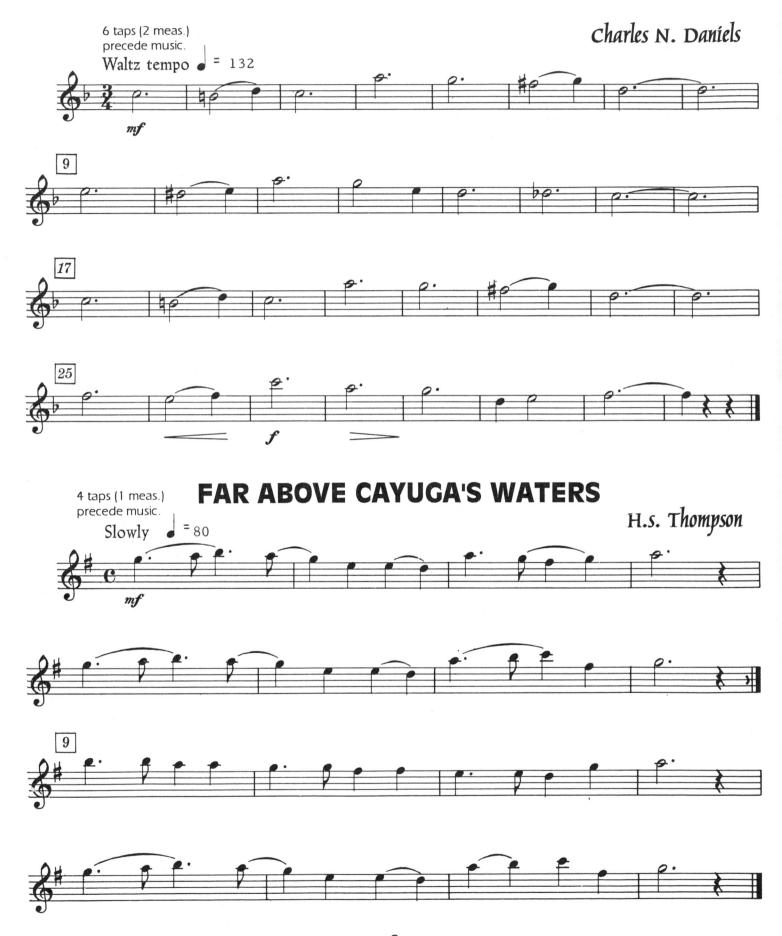

FAR ABOVE CAYUGA'S WATERS

H.S. Thompson

SPANISH GUITAR

College Song

CARELESS LOVE

WHEN THE SAINTS GO MARCHING IN

LITTLE BROWN JUG

BLUES IN E-FLAT

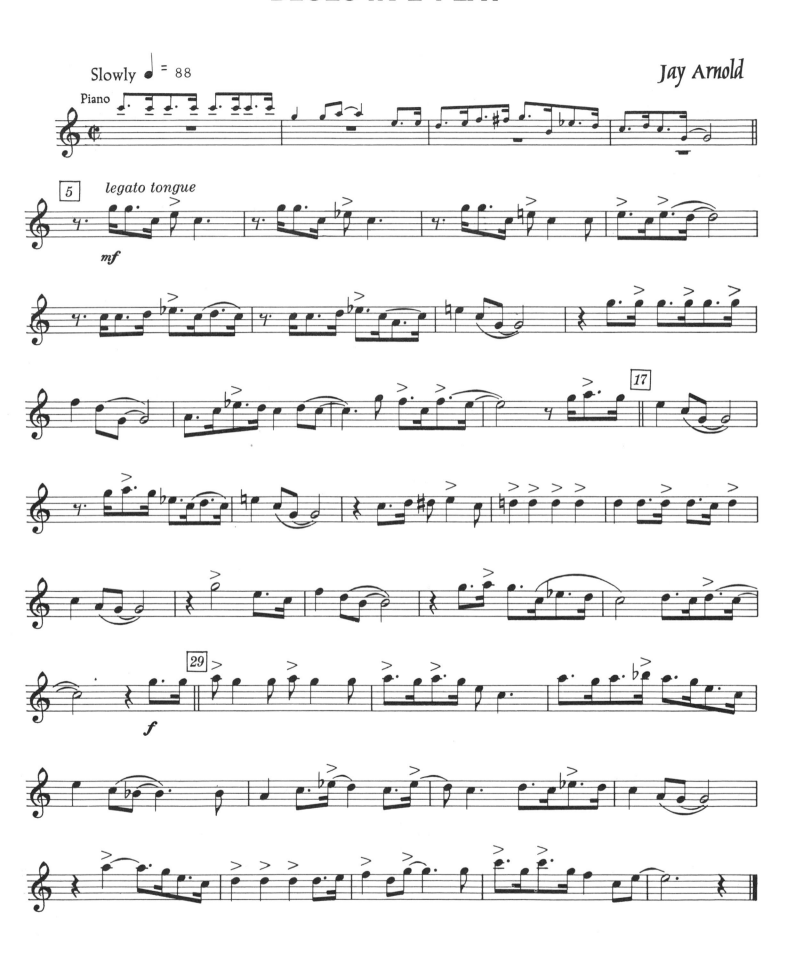

HELLO! MA BABY

Howard and Emerson

BLACK IS THE COLOR OF MY TRUE LOVE'S HAIR

JESU, JOY OF MAN'S DESIRING

J.S. Bach

H. M. S. PINAFORE

Sir Arthur Sullivan

PETER AND THE WOLF

THE HIGH SCHOOL CADETS

MANHATTAN BEACH

THE RIFLE REGIMENT

John Philip Sousa

THE COSSACK

Traditional Russian Melody

RECRUITING SONG
from "GYPSY BARON"

Johann Strauss

THEME FROM "MOLDAU"

Bedrich Smetana

MELODY FROM "PRINCE IGOR"

Alexander Borodin

THE YOUNG PRINCE AND THE YOUNG PRINCESS

N. Rimsky-Korsakoff

SCENE FROM "BLUEBEARD"

SCHEHERAZADE

from "ALBUM FOR THE YOUNG"

Robert Schumann

THE STARS AND STRIPES FOREVER

John Philip Sousa

TOREADOR SONG

from "CARMEN"

G. Bizet

BERCEUSE
from "L'OISEAU DE FEU"

Igor Stravinsky

NOCTURNE

Felix Mendelssohn

5 taps (1⅔ meas.) precede music.
Andante tranquillo ♩ = 72

poco ritard.

30

MODERATO CON MOTO
from 'CLARINET SONATA, Op. 120"

Johannes Brahms

VALSE NOBLE

Franz Schubert

IN DULCI JUBILO

J.S. Bach

CHORALE No.83

J.S. Bach